THE TIMES OF INDIA

FACT OF THE MATTER

FACT IS STRANGER THAN FICTION

Times Group Books

BOOKS AS MEDIA

Fact of the Matter

First published in 2008

by

Bennett, Coleman & Co., Ltd.
7, Bahadur Shah Zafar Marg
New Delhi-110002

Compiled by : Times Syndication Services
Edit, Design & Production : Times Group Books
Printed and bound by : Cirrus Graphics P. Ltd.

ISBN 978-81-89906-12-2

From the pages of History 5
Exploring Geography 41
Of Films and Flicks 63
Decoding the Human Body 79
Into the Animal Kingdom 117
Plant Surprises 155
Miscellaneous Factsheet 167

CONTENTS

Fact is stranger than fiction. Read this book and you'll know why!

Packed with factoids from history, biology, geography and a host of other subjects, this book unravels the unknown for you. Quirky facts, interesting facts, quick facts, useful facts, this book has them all.

If you're on the move and ready for some light reading, this book is a must. Go ahead...explore!

Facts and figures in this book have been culled out from a column by the same name that appears regularly in Delhi Times, a Times of India supplement.

FROM THE PAGES OF HISTORY

Mayonnaise is said to be the invention of the French chef of the Duke de Richelieu in 1756. While the Duke was defeating the British at Port Mahon, his chef was creating a victory feast that included a sauce made of cream and eggs. When the chef realised that there was no cream in the kitchen, he improvised, substituting olive oil for the cream. A new culinary masterpiece was born, and the chef named it "Mahonnaise" in honour of the Duke's victory.

In ancient Egypt, onions were an object of worship. They symbolised eternity for those who grew them in their garden. The anatomy of the onion suggested a circle within another circle and this structure symbolised eternal life.

William Henry Harrison served the shortest term of any US president. He served only 32 days, from March 4 to April 4, 1841. He fell ill with pneumonia shortly after his inauguration and never recovered.

David Modersbach and his four-year-old son drove from California to Argentina in a station wagon that ran on recycled vegetable oil.

Did you know that the Japanese construction company, Kongro Gumi, has been owned and operated by members of only the Kongo family since it was founded in the year 578 AD?

New Year's Day was April 1. Later, when the Church changed the calendar, they also changed the date. But some people continued using April 1 as the date of the new year. They were referred to as "April Fools".

Beethoven, who was a coffee lover, was extremely particular about his coffee. He always counted 60 beans in each cup when he prepared his brew.

Goethe could only write if he had an apple rotting in the drawer of his desk.

One time ruler of Egypt, Mohammed Ali, once created two infantry regiments made up entirely of one-eyed soldiers.

The ancient Egyptians recommended mixing half an onion with beer foam as a way of warding off death.

Before air conditioning was invented, white cotton slipcovers were put on furniture to keep the air cool.

The oldest individual to win a medal in the Olympic Games was Oscar Swahn. Oscar won a silver medal in shooting for Sweden in the year 1920. He was 72 years old at the time.

After his death, Alexander the Great's remains were preserved in a huge crock of honey. Among the ancient Egyptians, it was common practice to bury the dead in this manner.

Leonardo Da Vinci began painting the Monalisa in 1503. He was still working on the painting when he came to France in 1516. He finished it three years later, just before he died. The painting has remained in France ever since.

The earliest known appearance of the word "hello" in print is in a letter written by Thomas Edison dated August 15, 1877. He suggested that the word should be used to answer the telephone. "Hello" is an alteration of the much older word "Hollo".

Louis Pasteur, whose work on wine, vinegar and beer led to pasteurization, had an obsessive fear of dirt and infection. He refused to shake hands and carefully wiped plate and glass before dining.

Victorian publications never dared show a bed in any of their advertisements. When illustrations of the bedroom were required, the bed itself was hidden by curtains.

In the French court of Louis XI, the fine ladies lived mainly on soup because they believed that excessive chewing would cause them to develop premature facial wrinkles.

Voltaire considered Shakespeare's works so deplorable that he referred to the Bard as "that drunken fool".

The custom of saying "bless you" when someone sneezes was first used by the Greeks who believed that breath was the essence of life and when you sneeze, a part of your life is escaping. By saying this, the speaker is protecting the sneezer from evil spirits.

The Ottoman Empire once had seven emperors in seven months. They died of (in order): burning, choking, drowning, stabbing, heart failure, poisoning and being thrown from a horse.

The term "devil's advocate" comes from the Roman Catholic Church. When deciding if someone should be sainted, a devil's advocate is appointed to give an alternative view.

In the late 19th century, millions of human mummies were used as fuel for locomotives in Egypt where wood and coal were scarce, but mummies plentiful.

In the 1700s, European women achieved a pale complexion by eating "Arsenic Complexion Wafers" actually made with the poison.

Soap was considered a frivolous luxury of the British aristocracy from the early 1700s until 1862, and there was a tax on those who used it in England.

Tablecloths were originally meant to serve as towels with which guests could wipe their hands and faces after dinner.

Bolivia holds the record for the country with the highest turnovers in governments. Since 1825, Bolivia has had almost 200 governments.

Queen Lydia Liliuokalani was the last reigning monarch of the Hawaiian Islands. She was also the only queen the United States ever had.

Adolf Hitler wanted to be an architect, but he failed to clear the entrance exam at the School of Architecture in Vienna.

In ancient Greece, tossing an apple to a girl was the traditional proposal for marriage. Catching it meant she accepted.

Mata Hari's real name was Margaretha Zelle. She took the stage name Mata Hari when she became an exotic dancer, prior to becoming a spy during World War I.

Thomas Edison's first major invention was the quadruplex telegraph. Unlike other telegraphs at the time, it could send four messages at the same time over one wire.

In 1945, Percy Spencer discovered that when popcorn was placed under microwave energy, it popped. This led to many experiments with other foods, and ultimately, the birth of the microwave oven.

February 18, 1930 marks the first flight by a cow in an airplane. Elm Farm Ollie, while being watched by reporters, produced milk that was put into containers and parachuted over St Louis, Missouri, USA.

St Bernard of Menthon, who built way stations for tired medieval travellers in the Alps, is the patron saint of mountain climbers. The dog breed was also named after St Bernard.

Centuries ago, purchasing real estate often required having one or more limbs amputated in order to prevent the purchaser from running away to avoid repayment of the loan. Hence, an expensive purchase was said to cost "an arm and a leg."

Clans of long ago that wanted to get rid of their unwanted people without killing them, used to burn their houses down — hence the expression "to get fired".

EXPLORING GEOGRAPHY

The average hurricane generates energy which is roughly equal to 40,020 megaton bombs exploding in one day. This is the equivalent of all the electrical energy used in the United States for 6 months.

A small asteroid exploded in the air in 1908 near River Tunguska in Siberia. The resulting shock wave flattened 800 square miles of forest. The detonation's force was estimated to have been 1,000 times greater than the Hiroshima bomb.

There is so much moisture in the air that if all were to condense and fall, there would be up to an additional three inches of water added to the earth's surface.

Quito in Ecuador, South America, is said to have the most pleasant climate in the world. It is called the "Land of Eternal Spring". The temperature rarely drops below 46 degrees Fahrenheit during the night or exceeds 72 degrees Fahrenheit during the day.

Antarctica is 98% ice, 2% barren rock. The average thickness of the ice sheet is 7,200 feet. This amounts to 90% of all the ice and 70% of all the fresh water in the world. If the ice cap were to melt, the sea level would rise by an average of 230 feet.

The flag of Philippines is the only national flag that is flown differently during times of peace and war. A portion of the flag is blue, while the other is red. The blue portion is flown on top in times of peace and the red portion is flown on top during war time.

The Red Sea got its name from the extensive blooms of algae that, upon dying, turn the sea's normally intense blue-green waters to red.

Antarctica is the only continent without reptiles or snakes.

The Salto Alto (Angel Falls) in Venezuela is the highest waterfall known. It is more than twenty times higher than Niagara Falls.

Without any greenhouse effect, Earth would be cold and lifeless with an average temperature of -17.5 degrees Celsius.

The amount of garbage that is dumped in the world's oceans annually, is three times the weight of fish that is caught from the oceans.

Jupiter is two and a half times larger than all the other planets, satellites, asteroids and comets of our solar system combined.

It is estimated that a plastic container can resist decomposition for as long as 50,000 years.

Finland has the greatest number of islands in the world — 1,79,584.

More water flows over Niagara Falls every year than over any other falls on earth.

An iceberg contains more heat than a lit match.

The lowest temperature ever recorded in the world was 129 degrees below zero at Vostok, Antarctica, on July 21, 1983.

All the moons of the solar system are named after Greek and Roman mythological characters, except for the moons of Uranus, which are named after Shakespearean characters.

The highest temperature ever recorded on Earth was 136.4 degrees Fahrenheit at Al'Aziziyah, Libya, in 1922.

If all the salt were to be extracted from the Earth's oceans, you would have enough salt to cover all the continents five feet deep.

The South Pole is actually a desert environment, averaging about the same amount of monthly rainfall as the Sahara Desert.

Mercury has been known since the third millennium BC. The Greeks gave it two names — Apollo, for its apparition as a morning star, and Hermes, as an evening star. Greek astronomers knew, however, that the two names referred to the same body.

The sun burns 9 million tones of gas a second. At this rate, it has been estimated that it will burn out in another 10 billion years.

97 per cent of earth's water is not fit for drinking.

Rubies and sapphires are made of corundum — the hardest known rock on Earth after the diamond, which was first found in India 4,000 years back.

Tsunamis travel as fast as jet planes.

OF FILMS AND FLICKS

Film director DW Griffith invented false eyelashes while he was making the 1916 epic, "Intolerance". He wanted actress Seena Owen to have lashes that brushed her cheeks.

The longest Hollywood kiss was from the 1941 film, *You're in the Army Now*. It lasted for three minutes and three seconds.

Kevin Costner auditioned 3 times for the co-starring role of the ex-con that eventually went to Nicolas Cage in the offbeat comedy, Raising Arizona (1987).

At age 14, Tom Cruise enrolled in a seminary to become a priest but dropped out after one year.

Four hundred fifty yards of silk and lace were used to make Grace Kelly's wedding gown for her 1956 marriage to Prince Rainier of Monaco.

We are all used to seeing sequels and trilogies these days. But did you know that King Kong was the first movie to have its sequel (Son of King) released in the same year (1933)?

Hollywood actress Joan Crawford had her back teeth removed to make her cheekbones more prominent.

Chocolate syrup was used as blood in the famous 45-second shower scene in Alfred Hitchcock's movie Psycho.

Napolean Bonaparte is the historical figure most often portrayed in movies. He has been featured in 194 movies while Jesus Christ featured in 152 and Abraham Lincoln in 137 movies.

In James Bond movies, the armourer who supplies Bond with all his gadgets, is referred to as Q. The Q stands for "Quartermaster".

Manorama, an Indian comic actress, has played the maximum leading roles in film history. Starting in 1958, she had appeared in her one-thousandth movie by 1985.

Bruce Lee was so fast that they actually had to slow a film down so you could see his moves. That is the opposite of the norm.

Several of the Bond girls — Ursula Andress, Shirley Eaton, Eunice Gayson and Claudine Auger — were unable to match an alluring voice to their sexy figures. Their lines were dubbed by aspiring actress Nikki Van Der Zyl, who later left Hollywood to work as a barrister.

In 1888, Hollywood was founded by Harvey and Daeida Wilcox, who named the city after their summer home in Chicago.

Hollywood actor Bruce Willis was expelled during his senior year of high school after being blamed for a racial disturbance. He was only permitted to graduate because his father hired an attorney to get him reinstated.

Did you know? The first couple to be shown in bed together on prime time television were Fred and Wilma Flintstone.

DECODING THE HUMAN BODY

Did you know that the brain of an average adult male weighs 1,375 gm. And that the size of the human brain is not indicative of the intelligence quotient of man? The brain of Russian novelist Turgenev weighed 2021 gm, that of

Bismark weighed 1807 gm, while that of French statesman Gambetta was only 1294 gm. Einstein's brain was of average size but he was the brightest of them all.

Beards are the fastest growing hair on the human body. If the average man never trimmed his beard, it would grow to nearly thirty feet long in his lifetime.

One quarter of the bones in your body are in your feet.

Watching an hour-long soap opera burns more calories than watching a three-hour baseball game.

During your lifetime, you'll eat about 60,000 pounds of food. That's the weight of about six elephants.

A baby is born with 300 bones but by adulthood, only 206 are left in the body.

Sweat itself is odourless. Only when combined with bacteria, does it become smelly. Sweat is composed of water, sodium chloride, potassium salts, urea and lactic acid.

A man named Charles Osborne had hiccups for approximately 69 years.

Studies have shown that putting on slow background music can make a person eat food at a slower rate.

A foetus that is four months old, will become startled and turn away if any kind of light is flashed on the mother's stomach.

The only part of the human body that has no blood supply is the cornea. It takes its oxygen directly from the air.

When a person dies, hearing is generally the last sense to go. The first sense lost is usually sight. Then follows taste, smell and touch.

The easiest sounds for the human ear to hear, and those which carry best when pronounced are, in order, "ah", "aw", "eh" and "oo".

If you sneeze too hard, you can fracture a rib. If you try to suppress a sneeze, you can rupture a blood vessel in your head or neck and die. If you keep your eyes open by force, they can pop out.

Chocolate contains phenylethylamine (PEA), a natural substance that is reputed to stimulate the very same reaction in the body as falling in love does.

It has been proved that apples are more effective than caffeine at keeping people awake at night. This fruit contains a chemical that's stronger than caffeine.

The average human body contains enough iron to make a 3-inch nail, sulphur to kill all fleas on an average dog, carbon to make 900 pencils and potassium to fire a toy cannon.

Babies' eyes do not produce tears until the baby is approximately six to eight weeks old. The tear glands are not formed till then.

Humans shed about 600,000 particles of skin every hour — about 1.5 pounds a year. By 70 years of age, an average person will have lost 105 pounds of skin.

If you yelled for eight years, seven months and six days, you would have produced enough sound energy to heat one cup of coffee.

An apple, potato and onion all taste the same if you eat them with your nose plugged.

One has to eat 11 pounds of potatoes to put on one pound of weight — a potato has no more calories than an apple.

The average brain comprises 2 per cent of a person's total body weight. Yet, it requires 25 per cent of all oxygen used by the body, as opposed to 12 per cent used by the kidneys and 7 per cent by the heart.

An average woman has 17 square feet of skin. When a woman is in her ninth month of pregnancy, she has 18.5 square feet of skin.

Coughing can cause air to move through your windpipe faster than the speed of sound — over a thousand feet per second.

It takes food seven seconds to go from the mouth to the stomach via the oesophagus.

An average human blinks his eyes 6,205,000 times per year.

If all the blood vessels in your body were laid end to end, they would reach about 60,000 miles.

An average human produces a quart of saliva a day or 10,000 gallons in a lifetime.

Our stomach has to produce a new layer of mucus every two weeks or it will digest itself.

Your nose can identify upto 10,000 different odours.

Did you know that the average adult will stand around 0.5 inches taller in the morning than in the evening due to the slight cartilage compression that happens over the course of a day?

So where do you stand?

On an average, a person's weight drops by 300 gm each night.

The average person has at least seven dreams a night.

About 2/3rd of your body is made of water.

It takes the interaction of 72 different muscles to produce human speech.

Your hair grows about half inch per month and will grow faster in the summer than in the winter.

The two most common surgeries are biopsies and caesarean sections.

Babies are born without kneecaps. They don't appear until the child reaches 2-6 years of age.

Every two thousand frowns create one wrinkle on your face.

Dragonflies can travel at a speed of 60 mph.

A diet high in fat is said to impede memory.

Just like your fingers, your tongue has its own unique print, different from all others in the world.

The tongue is the strongest muscle in the body.

Nutmeg is extremely poisonous if injected intravenously.

On an average, a person will blink over 10,000 times a day

The greatest recorded number of children that have been given birth by one mother is 69! She gave birth to 16 pairs of twins, seven sets of triplets and 4 sets of quadruplets.

The velocity of your cough can be up to 60 mph.

Sneezes can reach up to 100 mph.

Each day, we lose anywhere between 10,000 to 100,000 brain cells.

A beard grows an average of 140 mm a year.

Banging your head against a wall will use roughly 150 calories an hour.

You use an average of 43 muscles to frown, as against an average of 17 muscles that you use to smile.

Each square inch of human skin consists of twenty feet of blood vessels.

The tooth is the only part of the human body that can't repair itself.

INTO THE ANIMAL KINGDOM

The bumblebee does not die when it stings. It can sting again and again. In bumblebee hives, the entire colony except for the queen, dies at the end of each summer. Each year, an entirely new colony of bees must be produced.

Did you know that the human tongue constitutes only capillaries and muscles? And that it tastes bitter things with the taste buds towards the back? Salty and pungent flavours are detected by the middle of the tongue and sweet flavours by the tip.

The blue whale is the loudest animal on earth. The call of the blue whale reaches levels up to 188 decibels. This extraordinarily loud whistle can be heard for hundreds of miles under water. The second loudest animal on earth is the howler monkey.

Elephant tusks grow throughout an elephant's life and can weigh more than 200 pounds. Among Asian elephants, only the males have tusks. Both sexes of African elephants have tusks.

Elephants only walk on their tip toes. This is because the back of their foot is made of complete fat. Their feet have no bones to give them support at the back.

The oldest known goldfish lived to 41 years of age. Its name was Fred.

Rats can swim for half a mile without resting, and they can tread water for three days straight.

Mussels can thrive in polluted water because of an inborn ability to purify bacteria, fungi and viruses.

Weighing approximately 6 kg at birth, a baby caribou will double its weight in just 10 days.

The black bear is not always black. It can be brown, cinnamon, yellow and sometimes, a bluish colour.

When a shrimp is born, it is male, and it gradually evolves to female as it matures.

Antlers and horns are not the same. Horns grow throughout an animal's life and are found on both the male and female of a species. Antlers, composed of a different chemical substance, are shed every year.

Grey whales migrate more than 19,000 km each year, farther than any other mammal.

The average cow spends 13 hours a day lying down.

Mother prairie dogs will nurse their young only while underground in the safety of the burrow. If an infant tries to suckle above ground, the mother will slap it.

The Egyptian vulture, a white bird about the size of a raven, throws stones with its beak to open ostrich eggs to eat. This bird is one of the very few animals that, like man, manipulates objects as tools.

The bombardier beetle, when disturbed, defends itself by emitting a series of explosions, sometimes setting four or five in succession. The noises sound like miniature popgun blasts and are followed by a cloud of reddish-coloured, vile-smelling fluid.

Alligators and old people have something in common, at least auditorily. They can hear notes only up to 4,000 vibrations a second.

The first chimpanzee to travel into space was named Ham. He got the name from the laboratory he was raised in. Ham flew in a space capsule in 1961. His trip also proved that space travel was safe for animals.

The largest known egg ever laid by a creature was that of the extinct Aepyornis of Madagascar. The egg was 9.5 inches long. It had a volume of 2.35 gallons.

The world chicken population is more than double the human population, while the world cattle population outnumbers the population of China.

Goldfish have a memory span of about 3-5 seconds. That's why you can leave them in a small jar and they won't get bored. You can also overfeed them till they die.

Tunas will suffocate if they ever stop swimming. They need a continual flow of water across their gills to breathe, even while they are resting.

If a cat falls off the 7th floor of a building, it has about 30 percent less chance of surviving than a cat that falls off the 20th floor. It supposedly takes about 8 floors for the cat to realize what is occurring, relax and correct itself.

Mosquito repellents do not actually repel. They simply hide you. The spray blocks the mosquito's sensors so they don't know you're there.

A common honeybee kills more people worldwide than all the poisonous snakes combined.

Sharks apparently are the only animals that never get sick. As far as is known, they are immune to every known disease including cancer.

Pet parrots can eat virtually any food eaten by humans except for chocolate because it is highly toxic and can be fatal for the parrot.

When a predator is chasing an impala, a type of antelope, it runs in a zigzag formation, jumping as high as 3 metres.

In 1958, the Crayola crayon colour "Prussian Blue" was changed to "Midnight Blue" at the behest of teachers as kids could not relate to Prussian history.

In 1997, the record for highest skydive by a dog at 4,572 feet, was set by a dog named Brutus.

Biologists have discovered that cockroaches can change course as many as 25 times in one second, making them the most nimble animals known.

Elephants are the only animals that can't jump.

Butterflies taste with their feet.

Mallard nests are sometimes built at a height of 40 feet above the ground. Surprisingly, when leaving their nests for the first time, chicks are very rarely hurt due to falling to the ground.

The Alaskan moose is the largest deer in the world. Its maximum height can sometimes exceed seven feet and, when fully grown, it weighs up to 1,800 pounds.

Cats have over 100 vocal sounds, whereas dogs have only 10.

There are some 50 different species of sea snakes, and all of them are venomous. They thrive in abundance along the coast from the Persian Gulf to Japan and around Australia. Their venom is ten times as virulent as that of the cobra.

Jelly fish are considered a delicacy by many cultures. After they have been dried and de-salted, they reportedly are not only delicious, but low in fat, calories and salt and rich in nutrients.

It takes 110 domestic silkworm cocoons to make a man's tie and 630 to make a woman's blouse.

A spider's silk is stronger than steel.

Australian scientists have identified some species of baby spiders that bite mothers and slowly dine on them over a period of weeks. The researchers hypothesize the material sacrifice keeps the young from eating one another.

Due to a retinal adaptation that reflects light back to the retina, the night vision of tigers is six times better than humans.

Cats have no ability to taste sweet things.

a crocodile cannot stick its tongue out.

a group of kangaroos is called a mob.

did you know that a dragon fly has a lifespan of just 24 hours?

PLANT SURPRISES

There are more than 700 species of plants that grow in USA and have been identified as dangerous if eaten. Among them are some that are commonly favoured by gardeners: buttercups, daffodils, lily of the valley, sweet peas, oleander etc.

The African baobab tree can have a circumference as large as 100 feet. One such tree in Zimbabwe is so wide that the hollowed-out trunk serves as a shelter at a bus stop, with a capacity to hold as many as 40 people.

When potatoes first appeared in Europe in the seventeenth century, it was thought that they were disgusting, and they were blamed for starting outbreaks of leprosy and syphilis. As late as 1720 in America, eating potatoes was believed to shorten a person's life.

Willow bark, which provides the salicylic acid from which aspirin was originally synthesized, has been used as a painkiller ever since the Greeks discovered its therapeutic power nearly 2,500 years ago.

An acre of trees can remove about 13 tons of dust and gases every year from the surrounding environment.

Oak trees are struck by lightning more often than any other tree. It has been theorized, this is one reason that the ancient Greeks considered oak trees sacred to Zeus, God of thunder and lighting.

Some farmers in Japan have learned to grow their watermelons into a square shape. They did this to conserve shelf space.

The oldest living thing in existence is not a giant redwood, but a bristle cone pine in the White Mountains of California, dated to be aged 4,600 years old.

The largest single flower is the Rafflesia or "corpse flower". They are generally three feet in diameter with the record being 42 inches.

The angle between the main branches of a tree and its trunk remains constant in each species — and this same angle is found between the principal vein of the tree's leaves and all its subsidiary branching veins.

Pollen never deteriorates. It is one of the few natural substances that lasts indefinitely.

MISCELLANEOUS FACTSHEET

In 1982, a high school student from Los Angeles, California unscrambled the Rubik's Cube in 22.95 seconds.

The average lead pencil can draw a line that is almost 35 miles long and using which you can write almost 50,000 words in English. Now imagine an eraser that could match it!

The first vending machines in the United States were installed on New York City train platforms in 1888 and dispensed chewing gum.

Asthma and Isthmi are the only six-letter words in English language that begin and end with a vowel. Another surprising aspect is that they have no other vowel in between them.

Almost is the longest commonly used word in the English language, with all the letters in alphabetical order.

Dueling is legal in Paraguay as long as both parties are registered blood donors.

More Monopoly money is printed yearly than real money throughout the world.

A whip makes a cracking sound because its tip moves faster than the speed of sound.

The three best known Western names in China: Jesus Christ, Richard Nixon and Elvis Presley.

No word in the English language rhymes with month, orange, silver and purple.

Leonardo da Vinci invented the scissors.

To an observer standing on Pluto, the Sun would appear no brighter than Venus appears in our evening sky.

The largest employer in the world is the Indian Railways. It employs over 1.6 million people!

In England, the Speaker of the House is not allowed to speak.

Nanotechnology has produced a guitar no bigger than a blood cell. The guitar, 10 micrometers long, has six strummable strings.

In Japan, it is considered extremely impolite to pour one's own drink when eating with others — you pour your companion's drink and your companion pours yours. On the other hand, it is considered ok to make loud slurping sounds when eating noodles.

There are over 375 organisations around the world devoted to Sherlock Holmes. The largest group is the Japan Sherlock Holmes Club, with over 1,200 members.

Sending red Christmas cards to anyone in Japan constitutes bad etiquette, since funeral notices there are customarily printed in red.

The word "dude" was coined by Oscar Wilde and his friends. It is a combination of the words "duds" and "attitude".

A standard garden hose can put out as much as 74 litres of water per minute. A hose left on by mistake can waste as much as 1,03,600 litres in just 24 hours.

Reportedly, Louisa May Alcott didn't want to write her classic novel, Little Women. She despised young girls and wrote the bestseller for the money.

Every year, surgical tools are left in approximately 1,500 patients in the USA. Fatter patients are more prone to having a surgical tool left inside them due to the additional amount of space in their bodies.

The Concorde holds two world speed records for commercial flights. In 1992, it circled the globe from east to west in 32 hours, 49 minutes and three seconds. Three years later, it flew west to east in 31 hours, 27 minutes and 49 seconds.

One gift-giving taboo in China is the giving of straw sandals, which are associated with funerals, and therefore considered to bring bad luck.

The main library at Indiana University, USA, sinks over an inch every year because when it was built, engineers failed to take into account the weight of all the books that would occupy the building.

The world's largest book, Bhutan: A Visual Odyssey, is in a Chicago public library. The book measures five feet tall by seven feet wide when open. It weighs 133 pounds.

Fried chicken is the most popular meal ordered in sit-down restaurants in the US. The next in popularity are roast beef, spaghetti, turkey, baked ham and fried shrimp.

At the end of the Beatles' song "A Day in the Life", an ultrasonic whistle, audible only to dogs, was recorded by Paul McCartney for his Shetland sheepdog.

A balloon released into a jetstream would take two weeks to travel completely around the globe.

The phrase "sleep tight" originated when mattresses were set upon ropes woven through the bed frame. To remedy the sagging ropes, a bed key was used to tighten the rope.

If you put a raisin in a glass of champagne, it will keep floating to the top and sinking to the bottom.

Dog owners in Turin, Italy can be fined up to $650 if they don't walk their dog at least three times a day!

James Naismith invented basketball in 1891. He set out to invent a game to occupy students between the football and baseball seasons.

The name for Oz in the Wizard of Oz was thought up when the creator Frank Baum looked at his filing cabinet and saw A-N and O-Z.

The one physical act that's recognised in every known society is the shrug of shoulders to mean, "I don't know."

There are only four words in the English language which end in "-dous": tremendous, horrendous, stupendous and hazardous.

The expression "hat trick" comes from cricket, where at one time, if a player scored three consecutive wickets, he was awarded a hat.

Peanut oil is used in underwater cooking in submarines. Undersea fleets like it because it does not smoke unless heated above 450 degrees Fahrenheit and so, keeps the atmosphere within clear.

When airplanes were still a novel invention, seat belts for pilots were installed only after the consequences of their absence was observed to be fatal — several pilots fell to their deaths while flying upside down.

The English word "soup" comes from the word "sop", which means a slice of bread over which roast drippings are poured. The first evidence of soup being consumed dates back to 6,000 BC, the main ingredient being hippopotamus bones.

Emily Dickinson wrote more than nine hundred poems, of which only four were published during her lifetime.

The sentence "the quick brown fox jumps over the lazy dog" uses every letter in the English language.

Wine will spoil if exposed to light, hence the tinted bottles.

Airports that are at higher altitudes require a longer airstrip due to lower air density.

A vexillologist is an expert in the history of flags

A jiffy is an actual unit of time for 1/100th of a second.

The word "salary" is derived from the Latin word "salarium" referring to the salt allotment for soldiers in the Roman Army.

Beer was not sold in bottles until 1850. Before then, if you wanted beer, you had to bring it home from the local tavern in a bucket made especially for it.

The term "jeep" came from the abbreviation GP used in the army for the General Purpose vehicle.

The shortest war in history was between Zanzibar and England in 1896. Zanzibar surrendered in just 38 minutes.

Since steel expands when it gets hot, the Eiffel Tower is six inches taller in the summer than in the winter.